Fernando Sarráis

30 Tips
for a Happy Life

Fernando Sarráis

*   *   *

Fernando Sarráis, PhD in Medicine and Surgery from the University of Navarra (Spain) and Psychology major, is a qualified psychiatrist since 1998. In 2000 he worked as a Research Fellow at the Faculty of Medicine of the University of Ottawa (Canada). He is a Member of the Ethics Committee of the Clínica Universidad de Navarra (Spain) and Professor of the Master in Educational and Psychological Treatment since 2007.

He holds the Silver Medal of the University of Navarra for his 25 years of work as a professor of psychopathology and personality psychology; as well as for his work as a clinical consultant, carried out in the Department of Psychiatry and Medical Psychology of the Clínica Universidad de Navarra (Spain).

Author of *Temperament, Character and Personality* (TECONTE, 2016); *Understanding Affectivity* (TECONTE, 2017); *Dialogue* (TECONTE, 2018) and *Family in Harmony* (PALABRA, 2019).

*   *   *

Introduction

In the Western world, instances of mental illness are becoming more common and more severe. We see it in the extensive abuse of alcohol among young people, the so-called binges, the widespread consumption of drugs, especially cannabis. Depression and anxiety disorders are no longer rare as we witness in the generalized use of anti-depressants, narcotics and mood stabilizers. Coupled with the alarming increase in addictions – chemical substances, sports betting, new gadgets, pornography, or the spike in cases of gender violence, cyber-bullying and online mobbing.

On the other hand, we see a clear disproportion between the efforts people make to have a "perfect body", as opposed to a "perfect mind". This is shown by the high demand for tattoos, piercing, tanning and laser techniques for removing hair; the heightened interest in sport and fitness; cosmetics, styling, make-up and the importance of fashion, as well as plastic surgery for a perfect face and figure.

Methods to improve psychological well-being, however, are not in high demand. Although, together with the development of positive psychology, e.g., motivational books and videos, some methods such as mindfulness and techniques of relaxation and meditation have become popularized over the last thirty years.

Since there is little interest in having a healthy mind, the number of people who are stressed, frustrated, embittered, annoyed, worried, fearful, consumed with envy, jealousy and resentment, depressed or enslaved by one or more addictions is greater than ever.

A person's state of mind can have two extremes, either negative, which we will call "mind zero" or positive, the "perfect mind". Our affectivity (feelings and emotions) determines the mind. Negative feelings and emotions produce a negative reaction which causes suffering and bad behavior. Positive affectivity, however, makes us feel good and helps us behave well so that we feel calm, at peace and optimistic.

A person longs for a "perfect body" because of its physical attractiveness; positive physical qualities makes others like and admire us, gives us high self-esteem and makes us feel good.

Someone wants a "perfect mind" for psychological well-being, a kind of "psychological beauty" which means the will is in control of the feelings to prevent negative outcomes: such as frustrations, failures, mistakes, losses or hurt. These cause negative feelings and emotions such as fear, anger and sadness that displace and overwhelm the positive ones such as peace and joy, and the ability to recover these when they have been lost.

Just as, in order to have a perfect body, one must apply certain physical methods, so to have a "perfect mind", one needs certain psychological strategies which are not so well known, but ever more necessary to turn around the general deterioration in mental health. This book offers some brief psychological tips which many people have found useful.

Psychological tips

This is the main part of the book. Its aim is practical and complements the theoretical aspects set out in previous books in which I explained how psychology works: both the healthy and mature and the unhealthy and immature.

This long section contains 30 tips that will help the reader live a healthy mental life, be positive, and have a "perfect mind" while taking into account the negative situations in life which cause suffering.

It is not an exhaustive explanation of every possible psychological strategy, but a selection. Many are used spontaneously by people who want to avoid feeling bad, to keep up joyful spirits or to recover them when they lose them; in a word, to be happy in life. Most were discovered through intuition and learnt by trial and error. Some were learned from persons with more experience of life or from professional psychologists and psychiatrists. Others were found in books on self-improvement, and finally some were heard from experts on courses, workshops

or Internet videos on self-improvement thera-
pies.

The advice or strategies explained here vary in quality. They differ as to the difficulty in being used and understood; some are more effective than others. They are in no particular order since they cannot be grouped thematically. Most are useful for life in general, not just special situations.

1. *Unconditional love for oneself*

We humans are happy when we are with people who love us and make us feel loved. Everyone needs love and when we do not receive it, we yearn for it, with greater or lesser intensity. Every unsatisfied need, physical or emotional, produces discomfort and suffering. And the deeper the dissatisfaction, the greater the suffering.

Even people who love themselves need the love of others but to a lesser degree than those who don't love themselves since these have to receive from others all the love they need, which makes them emotionally dependent on others. This dependence reduces their freedom to be themselves, for fear of displeasing others and losing their affection. Happiness increases and diminishes in proportion to the amount of love received, but also to the degree of one's personal independence.

Both self love and affection from others are needed if one is to be happy but love of self is more important, as can be seen by the degree of wellbeing and lower risk of suffering mental disturbances in people who love themselves.

Since we all love what is good and being human is something good, it is better to love oneself as one is, a human being, albeit with defects and limitations. In other words, to love oneself unconditionally and try to improve. It is not right to want to be perfect in order to be able to love ourselves, since we will never reach the goal as we can always improve.

So, the best love is an unconditional love: a love for the person, which is independent of how he behaves and, which shows itself in the way we remain cheerful and at peace when we make a mistake, or hurt others. It means loving ourselves as we are, not for the good things we may do, though naturally, when we do good, we love ourselves more than when we do evil. The Christian commandment says: "love your neighbor as yourself", that is: unconditionally.

Unconditional love of self increases when the person improves since there is a direct relationship between the degree of goodness and the degree of love. Moreover, love always pushes us to try to improve the object of our love and love it more and more firmly.

Some people are perfectionists who love only an ideal or perfect being and are incapable of loving the person they are, or of loving others as they are. They require themselves and others to improve before they can be loved. This kind of love is conditional, unreliable and limited and cannot satisfy the need for affection and this causes them continual suffering.

Those who can only love themselves on condition, normally have deep feelings of inferiority because they are not the person they want to be.

They compare themselves with others, especially with those better than them and they project onto them the ideal they wish to be as a way of encouraging themselves to emulate these people, in the hope of one day being ideal so they can then love themselves and be loved. Hence, their lives are filled with envy and unhappiness because there is always someone nearby who is better. They blame themselves when they don't achieve their goals, which are usually unattainable. When they do achieve them, their satisfaction is short-lived because they immediately set themselves an even higher target which puts back into a situation of fear of failure and frustration.

Therefore, a basic element in the education of children or in the search for fulfillment in adult life has to be: an unconditional love for oneself. Parents are advised not to compare their children with others as a way of encouraging them to improve. Adults should avoid comparisons with others so they too can learn to love themselves as they are. We have to do things well, according to our talents, but we don't have to do them the same as others and we have to remember that to do things well we will have to do them badly many times first. Our goal is to improve, not to be the same or better than others.

2. A passion for the truth

Beauty, goodness and truth are qualities that everyone admires. People feel good when they encounter them. On the other hand, ugliness, evil and deception make us uncomfortable, frustrated, annoyed, sad, disgusted and cheated.

Truth is also known as authenticity. It satisfies the need of the intelligence to know reality as it is, in order to be able to decide how to act properly, be happy and contribute to the happiness of their loved ones. For this reason, truth brings feelings of security, confidence and peace, whereas ignorance, error and lies make human reason's need for truth more acute, and produce uncertainty, confusion, anxiety, fear of making mistakes and anger, especially when faced with deception.

People who are genuine and authentic receive esteem and affection from others and this makes them happy. Authenticity is a consequence of love of self, which leads one to seek the best for oneself, which is to know and love the truth, which in turn reinforces self-esteem. Therefore, it ought to be obvious that everyone should be sincere and genuine, but in everyday life the opposite often happens. Many people lie to themselves and others and give a false picture of who they are. The popular saying goes: Tell me what you boast of and I'll tell you what you lack.

The main reason for lying is the fear of being embarrassed or rejected by others and even by oneself. Fear is a negative emotion as it causes suffering and makes us run away, lie, become inordinately submissive or violent in defense of our position. Fear is found in nearly all mental disturbances, in the form of anxiety, distress and panic. So, passionate love for the truth, which we spoke of in the last section, is a good antidote for fighting our natural tendency to lie to avoid suffering.

Truth is closely allied to good and freedom. Someone who conquers the fear of suffering by telling the truth will overcome the difficulties that doing good involves and will be free and the master of himself. Without truth, goodness and freedom, one cannot be happy.

Someone who is prepared to lie to others and to himself out of fear of suffering will eventually end up doing evil in order to avoid suffering, and since the fear of suffering does not disappear if one tries to flee but instead increases, even to the point of phobia, that person will end up losing their freedom, which is a quality of the will, while fear is an emotion.

Fear is an act of the emotions which is innate and serves to warn us of dangers against our physical or psychological well-being, but reason must guide us as to which fears are useful and which must be rejected as they limit our freedom and stand in the way of our happiness. And it is our will that must fight against, remove or reduce them, thereby increasing our freedom. This means we have to face up to situations that make us suffer or frighten us, and accept the fear which makes us suffer. To do this again and again calls for a great love for truth, which motivates the will to conquer fear. In this way one grows in fortitude, by facing our fears.

This is easier if the struggle begins in childhood. Parents and educators have to firmly and consistently educate children in the virtue of sincerity. This means showing them the positive part that suffering plays in human life. It is important for educators to set a good example by being examples of sincerity and love for truth. They can do this by rewarding sincerity and sanctioning lying so that young people learn not to lie as a way of avoiding suffering.

3. Develop the habit of thinking

The act of thinking is the capacity of the human intelligence to know more about reality and discover new truths from truths already known and stored in the memory. This process is also called reasoning and reflection.

In order to do good and be good, it is necessary to know reality as it is, that is to know it truly. In this way one can love oneself and be loved by others, which is an essential condition for happiness.

Discovering the truth by oneself is more useful than learning it from others. Truth is discovered through reasoning, and by frequent reflection we can develop the capacity to think how we find the truth. Over the course of a lifetime, we will discover many truths and acquire knowledge in accordance with our intellectual capacity.

Reasoning requires time and effort, whereas it is more comfortable to ask others to think for us, find the truth and give us answers. When a person habitually does this, he becomes intellectually dependent on others and unstable in his convictions since he is so influenced by the ideas of those around him that he changes his mind frequently. And since one's way of thinking determines one's actions, his life will be erratic and confused, with a permanent feeling of emptiness and dissatisfaction. Personality psychologists of the school of phenomenology have qualified this type of person as inauthentic. The Swiss psychiatrist, Ludwig Binswanger (1881-1966) said that inauthentic people follow conventions and fail to exercise their own freedom. Instead, they just live a life of conformity with whatever others do. They copy what others do or say to avoid making life choices. In this way they avoid the anxiety that comes with making a mistake or the feelings of guilt that come when someone squanders their life.

Reason is the compass which guides us towards happiness. If it is not made use of, it atrophies and we are left with no other option but to imitate others. To avoid this, we have to overcome our laziness and make the effort to think, which is the only way to learn new things, to gain knowledge and prestige. Then we earn the admiration and love of others and consequently feel content and rightly proud of ourselves.

The habit of thinking must begin in childhood so as to take deep root. As in every learning experience, the ones who start the process are parents and teachers. These educators have to be convinced of the importance of developing a child's reasoning powers. In order to stimulate the thinking process of youngsters, they should ask them to explain the reasons why they do or do not do something. Before answering a question from a young person, it is good to ask their opinion and let them think it out for themselves, even if takes more time. Adults must be good models of rational beings, which means explaining: 1) the reason for each rule and penalty they establish; 2) the reason why they do or do not do a certain thing; 3) the reasons why they consider something good or bad, and 4) the reasons behind their opinions.

In this way, educators can teach youngsters to be rational. This will help them know themselves better and learn how to make use of their abilities to live a happy life and make those around them happy.

4. Become aware of yourself and act accordingly

Self-awareness is a psychological construct among the functions of the intelligence, the faculty by which we know the truth of things. It enables us to apprehend the realities of past, present and future; it implies knowing something with certainty or truthfulness. So, one can be aware of being in a fixed place at a fixed time (temporal-spatial orientation), aware of one's personal history such as having paid a bill the week before; aware of a future plan, such as a forthcoming job interview one day next month.

One can also be aware of interior realities: one's identity, age, civil status, profession or job; physiological needs: hunger, thirst, sleep, physical discomforts, aches and pains; one's ideas, attitudes and affections for oneself, others and the world at large, as well as social and environmental aspects of life.

This awareness can vary in intensity depending on the attention one gives to the contents of one's awareness, which in turn depends on physiological, emotional, motivational and social aspects.

Among introverts these contents are normally aspects of one's interior world: intellectual reflections, movements of the heart, expectations and plans that involve the imagination. Among extroverts the most usual contents are aspects of the outside world: things to be done, how to have a good time, how to get what I want, how to feel good and how to make others happy. Since most of us are somewhere in the middle, our awareness is a mixture of both.

Self-awareness is linked to our intelligence and will. When we want to know something or desire an object, it starts to appear more frequently in our mind. At times it may appear too often and cause anxiety or become obsessive. This gives rise to two types of sickness: obsessive-compulsive disorder (OCD) or anankastic personality disorder. In either case, the will of the person is unable to control the obsessive repetition of ideas.

There is also a close link between awareness, feelings and emotions. When a person becomes strongly aware of something they will be affected, positively or negatively. And vice-versa, when we feel strong emotions our conscience will bring to mind memories, thoughts and fantasies connected with those emotions. One way of remembering things of the past is to recreate those feelings, and these kinds of memories are more intense in people who are more emotional. For example, when a mother is worried about a child many things related with that child come to her mind.

Our consciousness is like a screen onto which are projected many things related to the person: physical and psychological needs, tendencies and motivations, affections, interests, plans and targets. Often it is difficult for the person to know: 1) their origin, relevance and importance; 2) their appropriateness and suitability; and 3) how long to allow them to remain. We need to develop habits of reflection and voluntary control of what appears in our mind so that it adds to our happiness rather than cause mental illness.

Having a correct understanding of oneself and one's surroundings depends largely on our upbringing. People's self-awareness varies, 1) some have an upright conscience, others, deformed; 2) some are realistic, others more imaginative; 3) some are practical, others have their head in the clouds; 4) some are self-centered, others think more of others. The contents of the conscience form the basis for this categorization.

Self-awareness is important because it contributes to our happiness. Happiness comes from being able to behave well freely, this makes us free and happy, which in turn makes us more attractive to others and enhances self-esteem. Humans are rational beings who use reason to know how to behave properly at any moment in order to be happy. Reason presents to the conscience its judgments on the reality of things and the goodness or otherwise of acts, and the person derives a feeling of happiness when he acts freely in accordance with his reason.

It can happen that after reason has presented its good ideas or judgments, alternative ideas generated by the memory or imagination appear, fed by our emotions. Sometimes these reinforce, but more often they oppose the ideas proposed by our reason, especially when they are difficult to achieve.

Common forms of opposition are: 1) doubts, since doubt stifles action; 2) difficulties, also a hindrance to action; and 3) arguments that try to persuade that it is not the right moment, better to wait. In fact, this means leaving things undone, but in a way that seems reasonable. This tension between reason and feelings in the conscience will be further discussed in the next section.

The best way to be happy and enjoy good mental health is to pay heed to the suggestions of reason in our conscience: "follow your conscience" as they say. But one also needs the strength of will to put the promptings of conscience into practice, as in expressions like: "act in conscience". If one doesn't act like this, one suffers remorse and sadness.

When we neglect duties, they keep appearing in the conscience spurred by the will, until they are fulfilled. Experience teaches that what is most tiring is to have things on your conscience; it weighs you down.

To derive the maximum benefit from one's conscience, one has to learn to trust it by following the suggestions planted there by our reason. Conduct and thinking are interconnected: "Either we live according to the way we think or we end up thinking according to the way we live."

Acting in conscience is not error-free, but when we make a mistake, our conscience will eventually point out the mistake to us and help us rectify. People whose conscience is well-formed will make fewer mistakes than those whose is not, but by following conscience, anyone can develop the habit of acting conscientiously by learning from one's mistakes.

By doing this a person can feel they are in charge of their life, even if they sometimes make mistakes. Some people have a pathological fear of making mistakes which leads them to rely on what others say or do. Such people are dependent on others and only feel secure and unafraid when they do what others say or do. This has to be avoided since each time we rely on others instead of ourselves, we lose a little more of our freedom and happiness.

In the same way that we train our hearing for music and languages, we can also fine-tune our attention to what our conscience is telling us so we can react quickly and habitually to its insinuations. We learn to trust our conscience as we come to understand the reasons for its promptings and realize that actions done in conscience are to our benefit.

For example, a certain person may come to mind, one may ask: why? It may be that we have not seen the person for a long time and ought to visit, we lent him a book we should get back or we owe him money and should pay. Once we carry out these suggestions of our conscience we feel better. Or, there may be no reason, though it can be a reminder to contact them to renew our relationship or an occasion to recall their friendship. Other times a duty comes into our conscience: to clean and tidy up, to study, to work, to put things in order, to have the car serviced, to make a doctor's appointment, to visit a relative, to greet someone on their birthday or anniversary, to keep quiet and be tactful, or to ask someone for forgiveness. Someone sensitive to the voice of conscience and in control of their actions will follow these reminders of conscience or at least make a note to do so at the first available moment without excuses or delays because if not, they know they risk forgetting it completely. Our feelings easily invent excuses, doubts and difficulties that discourage us from acting.

The one who doesn't follow the voice of conscience ends up a passive spectator, unaware of the contents of conscience. Whereas an average person who heeds the voice of conscience, will be effective, responsible and successful in life, will inspire confidence and admiration, and will feel at peace, self-assured and content. The one who disregards the voice of conscience is just the opposite and will end up being rejected by others, frustrated and dissatisfied.

5. Pay attention to interior dialogue

It is good to develop the habit of being aware of one's interior dialogue and channel it in line with reason and so as to arrive at true, good and helpful conclusions that enable us to have a beneficial, pleasant interior life that makes us and those around us feel good and inspire them with feelings of respect and affection.

Two parties take part in the interior dialogue: on the one side the head and the heart, and on the other, sensitivity and feelings.

Reason judges the right thing to do and the evil to avoid, as well as the duties to be fulfilled. It guides each one how to behave well and thus be good, well-liked and happy. But in order to follow the dictates of reason, the energy of the will is needed.

Our affectivity leads to behaviors that will produce positive feelings directly and immediately while sidelining those that produce negative feelings.

During childhood and adolescence, a person has stored up in his conscience a host of dialogues and 'dialectical' conflicts between the reasons of the head, and the impulses suggested by our feelings derived from the need to feel good. Depending which 'side' wins, this conflict produces three kinds of person: 1) those in whom the head is at the service of their feelings and desires — their behavior is temperamental and pleasure-seeking; 2) those whose feelings yield to reason — their behavior is cold, selfish and headstrong; 3) balanced and mature people whose mind and feelings are in harmony — their actions are rational and warm at the same time. We call this emotional intelligence. Each one of us belongs to one of these three types.

The relationship between head and heart develops with age and interior struggle and can improve or deteriorate according to the intensity of effort applied to understanding and controlling the dialogue between the two and monitoring its effect on our behavior.

As we shall see in greater detail in the section titled "Be critical of your feelings" it is advisable to be clear on how important it is to achieve a good balance between head and heart, a balance based on a hierarchy, because decisions are made by the mind and the will but with the assistance of the feelings and emotions at every moment.

Thus, an important goal of dialogue and interior struggle is to ensure that the constant attempts of the feelings to impose themselves on the mind do not succeed. Feelings are very powerful, as seen by the huge number of people who rely on their feelings and emotions to judge reality erroneously and then act wrongly for short-term satisfaction. These people end up thinking that their feelings are right without realizing they are the main source of subjectivism and distortion of reality. Feelings relate mainly to the present moment and so are very fickle, making individuals unstable, subjective and unrealistic. This makes them crash against reality and disagree with those who see reality differently. Consequently, such people who cause great suffering for others and themselves are condemned to loneliness and maladjustment to the world around them.

But it is negative feelings, such as fear, anger, sadness, shame, insecurity, envy, and resentment that are the greatest obstacle to the harmonious balance between head and heart, since positive feelings, such as peace and joy, make it easier for our reason to function logically and our will

to act freely and this is when the interior dialogue works best.

Feelings that are in harmony with reason
and will increase the vital energy of the person,
enabling him to be as he wants to be. Whereas
when they are at loggerheads they paralyze, and
this disordered dialogue leads a person in the opposite direction from where he wants to go.

Feelings and emotions do play a positive role,
they provide important information about reality,
but reason must then analyze how useful the information is in terms of our medium- and long-
term objectives. Our negative emotions may
tell us that there is a risk that reality may bring
suffering, but our reason may decide that the suffering is worthwhile to achieve the objective one
really wants (and that will make us happy). In
immature people and those with certain mental
illnesses, negative feelings are often so powerful
that they prevent the will from behaving in the
way right reason suggests. Positive feelings tell
someone that reality is safe and has elements that
are beautiful, good and genuine that he can enjoy. Thus, having positive feelings and emotions

at all times is the key to harmony between mind and heart. In social life, people who know how to agree and get along easily with others achieve more worthwhile and satisfactory targets (that make everyone happy). Something similar occurs when one attains a high level of mutual understanding and a low level of conflict between mind and heart, but this requires regular practice during childhood and adolescence. Parents and teachers have to ask youngsters why they acted in a certain way, especially in more important matters. In turn, young people need to analyze their interior motives, which usually originate in the mind, when they act well, or in their feelings when they do not. In this way they learn what lies at the root of their behavior and appreciate the need to understand and control their interior dialogue in order to become what they want to be and feel as they want to feel.

As said above, reason is the faculty that enables us to know the truth of things, allowing us to adapt well to reality, and judge correctly what we have to do at any given moment in order to be accepted and loved by others.

Feelings, particularly negative ones deceive our reason, since they try to convince it that it is mistaken or that what the mind thinks is true, is actually false, and that the real truth is what the feelings want. And so they try to convince the mind that duty is not compulsory: what is compulsory is to feel good here and now.

The one who learns how to love the truth passionately in childhood is immunized against deceitful feelings and his reason is more likely to dominate his interior dialogue. Therefore, an early upbringing in sincerity is essential. To learn to distinguish whether the contents of one's conscience come from the mind or from the feelings, we must first discern if they are logical and objectively good: good for oneself and others. The voice of reason is logical, true and good, whereas the feelings talk about what makes us feel good, but is not logical, and may even be bad for us. When the voice of conscience speaks logically and says things which make us feel well, then the person himself is speaking, that is to say reason and feelings are in mutual agreement. This is more likely to happen in older, mature people who have achieved the right harmony where the mind commands the heart without repressing the feelings. This interior harmony is like a well-coordinated orchestra, a pair of dancers in perfect step or a rider with a well-trained horse.

6. Convince yourself

One particular kind of interior debate consists in repeating to oneself time and time again how good it would be to do something, which the mind considers good for us or good for other people but which we never get round to doing because our feelings persuade us that it is too demanding.

The constant repetition of the idea makes it look as though the mind is trying to convince itself that it is good but since the opposition comes from the feelings, the goal of this insistent repetition is really to convince the feelings. When we say "convince yourself", what we really mean is "convince your heart."

This is a strategy many people use to coax their feelings to agree to actions which the mind has identified as worthwhile and necessary, which the Will acknowledges will bring happiness in the long term but which the feelings reject because the action may initially bring suffering.

Therefore, we use this strategy of persuasion to resolve the mind-heart conflict and the Will proposes to the emotions that it is willing to face a little suffering in the short term to obtain the greater benefit – joy and wellbeing – which will come. "No pain, no gain" as they say: if you want to be happy you must be prepared to make an effort and go through a bit of a hard time. This is the price we pay for worthwhile objectives which our feelings naturally reject. To overcome this resistance, it is good to develop the habit of "driving yourself a little crazy" because if you persevere, the time will come when feelings are won over, and that is the chance to make the effort to achieve something really worthwhile.

This strategy can be used in situations when sacrifices are needed to keep us physically or psychologically healthy; or facing family, social or work obligations, e.g. I have to reduce weight or stop smoking, play sports, get up early; I must use my phone less, study more, not do shoddy work, not get annoyed so often; or be more courageous and stand up for my friends, look after my family better and spend more time with the kids... These are all good, desirable outcomes because they make us happy, but they require effort and perseverance and acceptance of failure time and again, all of which makes us feel bad for a while and which our feelings therefore reject.

We have to be patient with ourselves and never throw in the towel as we try to convince ourselves that we need to struggle to hit worthwhile targets, though it may be tough going. So many people have stopped smoking after many failed attempts. Others have managed to lose weight, become organized, punctual, sincere and hard-working, learned to be more considerate after many years of thinking how beneficial it would be to do so.

By persevering in trying to win over one's feelings, it gradually gets easier and the emotions end up trusting reason once they realize that it's worth undergoing a bit of a hard time when afterwards one tastes the reward of feeling very good. It's like domesticating a pet. Once it's trained it's very gentle and its owner can treat it with a lot of affection.

Some people have fewer doubts because from very young they learned to resolve the conflicts between mind and heart in favour of the former. These are people with a psychological harmony that allows them to live a peaceful, cheerful life. This positive state of mind enables them to get the very best out of their Reason and Will. We call such people psychologically mature and they are well placed to live a happy life.

The opposite occurs with immature people; they experience frequent internal conflicts, which they resolve by trying to appease their feelings although their reason tells them they will feel worse in the end. Such people habitually have negative emotions and feelings because often the world does not allow them to do what they like or punishes them for not behaving normally. Hence, they are more likely to suffer mental illness and in the long term hurt themselves and everyone around them.

One should not confuse the strategy of "self-persuasion" with obsessiveness. Both involve repetitive mental actions, but the first is positive and the second is pathological because it hinders normal activity and torments the subject.

One kind of obsessiveness that is a negative character trait of moderate intensity and another is a symptom of a mental disorder known as obsessive-compulsive disorder. This is so intense that it makes the person fix their mind on one topic without ever coming to a conclusion, thereby freezing their behavior because they are unable to decide and incapable of action. While the driving force behind self-persuasion is the Will, obsessiveness is driven by fear: fear of making a mistake, of failing, of committing a sin, or doing something badly, causing harm, or anything that brings negative outcomes. Fear stifles reason, preventing it from choosing the best course of action.

7. Live in the present: today and now

Humans are teleological beings who live for goals that they enjoy and are happy with when they achieve them. The more worthwhile the goals are, the more we feel spurred to go for them. The more challenging they are, the more they satisfy us. But we have to work hard in the here and now, focusing our attention and energy to the task in hand which will bring us closer to our future goal.

Some people get easily distracted from the task in hand by memories of the past or thoughts about the future. Unless they make an effort to avoid this, they will not develop the willpower needed to focus and concentrate on the present. One common cause of distraction is the need to escape the present moment because it is hard and requires effort. Their lack of attention is a kind of blindness preventing them from seeing things as they are, so they escape into nostalgia. Other times they escape into the future, inventing fantasies in which everything is wonderful, and this helps lift their spirits. The pleasant feelings produced by the nostalgia and fantasies shield them from the unpleasant feelings of the daily grind and the uncertainty of reaching their current goals.

Sometimes the distractions of today are related to past sufferings which they have not accepted. These bring to mind traumatic events of the past and stimulate the mind to create preventive devices to avoid their recurrence. In this way they free themselves from fear which incites the mind to plan revenge or retaliation. Or they make the imagination build up images of future dangers, which spur the Reason to invent preventive devices to protect them from future suffering and conserve feelings of peace and safety.

If such people wish to be happy, they will have to: 1) strive to recover control of their interior world and put order in their conscience to avoid an invasion of past memories, especially negative ones which make it hard for their mind and will to function properly; 2) stop the invasion of fantasies, which distract them from focusing on the present, and leave them unprepared for a future quite contrary to their expectations.

Hence, if someone wants to have good mental health, he has to stop a negative past or future from embittering the present. He also has to prevent excessively negative reactions to things that happen to him because these have a stronger impact on the emotions than memories or fantasies. Some people, such as pessimists and the timid, have a negative personality, whose mental faculties (memory, imagination, perceptiveness, thinking habits and emotions) habitually function in a negative way. It is not logical to be like this and it is not something they would have freely chosen but it is a strategy they use to anticipate worst case scenarios to reduce the suffering they cause but since things are never so bad as they imagine, their anxiety is pointless, as in any case they cannot eliminate the possibility of something bad happening in the future.

If one is rational, it is obvious that the most logical thing is to try to be happy here and now because if we manage to do this in our present situation, we will be happy when tomorrow comes since we will have learned to remain cheerful in spite of adverse circumstances. This means learning to be positive, which implies learning not to be negative. Pessimism is a result of accumulated negative reactions to things that go wrong in our lives; these displace our positive feelings, the ones which make us optimistic. Optimism makes it easier to accept the present, rather than fleeing into an imaginary world where we can find comfort.

To manage to live in the present one must: 1) get used to not blaming oneself for past mistakes and let go so as to be able to live fully and positively in the present. The bad things of the past cannot be changed by brooding on them; it is enough to ask for forgiveness and resolve to improve if the mistakes were deliberate, and learn the lessons of the past in order to be able to live better in the present. This requires a continuous effort to drive negative memories out of one's conscience promptly and avoid complaining when we suffer, since this makes the suffering worse. 2) Give up the idea that we can design a future that matches our tastes and so avoid the things that can make us suffer. Many people are worried about the future because they fear things like personal failure, being made fun of, being abandoned, loneliness, humiliation, illness, financial problems, one's own death or that of a loved one. Worry is a form of fear that pushes a person to continually devise avoidance strategies, trying out imaginary solutions for all potential future setbacks. Fear brings suffering, anxious people suffer continually by trying to avoid future suffering. If this kind of people want to change, they have to learn how to face present difficulties so they can stop being afraid of the future, always imagining the worst and making the present a living hell. This is the only way they can live with peace and joy in the here and now. We can encourage them by reminding them that our future is what we make it, and what they have to do is 'be occupied but not pre-occupied' and do what has to be done right now. Responsible people know how 'to focus on what right Reason tells them', which are the things to do at any given moment and not leave for tomorrow what you can do today. If not, you won't do it tomorrow either but leave it for the day after. This kind of negligence guarantees that the evil we feared becomes a reality. Many people worry about the future and embitter the present when in fact what they ought to do is make others happy.

Human beings always dream of getting the things they like because thinking that once they do, they will be happy. This means choosing the right course of action at any given moment and then carrying it out without worrying about how it will turn out. How one works and how the job turns out are closely connected, but the important thing is the work, not how it turns out because the task itself may take many days, but the outcome is a matter of a moment. If we don't learn how to enjoy work in the hope of achieving the desired result, the uncertainty of the outcome will make us suffer. We can never be sure of how work will turn out or even if we will live to see the end result. What is quite certain is that we have to work for the outcome that will make us happy. But we must also learn how to enjoy the work of every day, since this helps us persevere. We have to accept that if we are not happy with today's situation when tomorrow comes around, we won't be happy either because there is bound to be another obstacle in the way. So, learning to be happy today regardless of the circumstances is the best guarantee that we will manage to be happy in future.

People who do what they have to do at each moment, without stopping to consider the cost, or if they like it or not, or if it will turn out well or not, manage to do many worthwhile, important things in their lifetime and win the favor of others for being responsible and trustworthy. Their achievements give them a rightful pride and they are at peace with themselves.

In recent years in the Western world, a psychological technique called mindfulness has become popular that advocates full awareness in the present moment. This attempts to reverse the widespread tendency to escape from the present.

To complete this section, I will comment briefly on attention deficit hyperactivity disorder (ADHD), which is a biological disorder that consists of a lack of activity in the cortex of the front lobe of the brain, specifically the orbitofrontal zone whose function is to program a person's actions, determine the consequences, prioritize actions and monitor behavior. People who suffer from this, especially in childhood and adolescence, find it biologically impossible to concentrate on the work in hand and get easily distracted by all kinds of stimuli around them. They have insufficient control over the impulses that generate their sensations and natural needs. This disorder has nothing to do with what we have explained so far, because this is a mental disorder, not a way of evading unpleasant feelings. This illness can improve with medication to activate the cerebral cortex.

8. "What the eye doesn't see, the heart doesn't grieve over."

This popular expression means that what you don't see doesn't affect you because you're not aware of it. In other words, what does not reach one's awareness has no emotional repercussions. Although the expression that heads this section speaks of eyes, we could also say 'What the ears do not hear, the heart doesn't grieve over' or

'What the mind doesn't think, the heart doesn't grieve over.'

One can avoid much grief by learning to distinguish between seeing and looking, listening and hearing, between a momentary distraction and a thought or reflection. Seeing and hearing produce sensations, but looking and listening produce perceptions, part of the process of knowing reality by analyzing what has been captured by the senses and grasping its significance and impact. This brings about a specific emotional response that may be positive or negative, more or less intense and lasting depending on the sensitivity of the person.

Regarding distraction and reflection, the first appears in one's conscience as an idea coming either from the Will, which seeks what is good and right, or from the feelings, which simply want to feel good. Reflection is an analysis and evaluation of an idea that appears in our conscience and produces an emotional response.

To have good mental health, we need to look, listen and reflect on what is beautiful, good and true because this makes us feel good (positive

affectivity) and enables us to behave well. Likewise, we have to cut short the opposite as this
makes us feel bad (negative affectivity).

Negative feelings and emotions predominate
in people who have negative affectivity; they
feel driven to do negative things and make others suffer too. The list of negative feelings is
very long: fear, anger, sadness, shame, hatred,
resentment, envy, jealousy, etc. However, the list
of positive feelings is shorter and can be reduced
to two: peace (calmness, freedom from anxiety,
restfulness, gentleness), and joy or cheerfulness.

Negative feelings make people behave in a
negative way in their thoughts, their memories,
their dreams and their conduct; this leads to even
more unhappiness in a vicious circle which can
produce mental disturbances: anxiety disorders,
phobias, obsessions, physiological effects or depression.

If this becomes a rooted habit it becomes impossible for the will to reject the negative contents of the consciousness and a long process of
mental rehabilitation will be needed to re-train
the will so the person can become positive again.

There are people whose mind is a warren of unhappy events which they try to assimilate to numb the pain. They avoid getting excited at positive events out of fear that they will be let down. And so, they take perverse pleasure in negative things, consoling themselves by saying: "Better the devil you know than the devil you don't."

It is well known that the media focus more on the bad than the good because evil sells better than good, and they sell what the public wants. One possible psychological explanation of this, in the news media and in the minds of people, is that misery loves company. When you feel bad, you suffer less if others are also having a hard time: the more people who suffer, the greater the consolation. This is not a logical reaction; it is not rational since the fact that others are in pain doesn't stop me from suffering; but enduring it alone is more painful because the feeling of loneliness implies that one is not loved, and love is the best balm to alleviate suffering. Hence the consolation that we get from having others around us suffer is not rational, it is emotional.

We all experience frustrations in our daily lives because 1) to do things well we first have to do them badly, and mistakes are frustrating; 2) problems crop up frequently and solving them is not easy and takes time; 3) living with others brings little frictions and frustrations; and 4) getting what we want is usually difficult. Frustrated people often think that the same or worse must be happening to others, so if everyone suffers, they don't feel alone, which makes things worse.

To forestall this negative attitude, we have to realize that we need to have some control over our thoughts and senses, particularly our sight and hearing, so as to defend ourselves from the impact of feelings caused by negative events. In the same way that people in dangerous jobs take measures of safety and hygiene at work to protect their health (use of helmets, harnesses, masks, special footwear), we all need to take safety measures of mental hygiene to protect our mental health, which means protecting our positive feelings (peace and cheerfulness), and avoiding listening, hearing and dwelling on negative things.

9. *Emotional independence from others*

Emotional independence means that when a person decides their conduct, as rational beings, they are free to follow the dictates of reason while taking into account their feelings and emotions, skills and abilities and the circumstances.

Some people habitually act by following the impulse of their emotions and feelings, despite their Reason telling them that such actions are inappropriate, incorrect or bad. These emotions usually come to the surface as a reaction to stimuli of a biological, psychological, physical or sociological nature. This reaction implies an emotional dependence on internal or external stimuli. When the emotional reactions produce an automatic behavioral response, we can say that the person has a dependent personality; this reduces his freedom, and subsequently, his capacity for happiness.

Children are emotionally dependent on their physiological needs, on stimuli from their environment and on their caregivers. Their personal development should aim to reduce this dependency, until they reach psychological maturity. Emotional independence and the freedom it confers are key characteristics of a mature, healthy individual.

Emotional independence can never be absolute because every human being is emotionally affected by physiological or environmental stimuli and conditioned by them. This applies especially to social stimuli owing to our need for the affection of others.

Psychological maturity is everyone's aim because it enables us to have a happy, healthy life. The mature person is emotionally independent, is able to act freely, and follows the will, which leads him along the right path marked out by reason. The Spanish psychiatrist, Enrique Rojas says that the ideal adult "is capable of being himself, of ignoring stereotypes and behaviors that have more to do with seeking approval than with self-expression."

Being afraid that others think badly of us and no longer love or respect us, is what makes us worry about how others judge our actions; this keep us in suspense until we are absolutely certain of their good opinion. But this kind of certainty is rare since we never really know what others think of us.

People with an inferiority complex need the esteem of others to feel appreciated and secure. They are highly emotionally dependent and cannot rid themselves of their concern for what others think of them. Thus, they are pressured into submitting to the opinions and wishes of others.

To free ourselves from others' opinions, we must first convince ourselves of that it is worthwhile doing so. We must rid our minds of every thought about what they think, have thought or will think. In this way we can get rid of the fear of being judged and rejected: "mind that doesn't think, heart that doesn't grieve". We avoid ending up as 'actors' who have to win over the audience continually and in the process lose the freedom to be ourselves. Being ourselves is indeed worthy of admiration since people tend to admire what is beautiful, good and authentic.

Not caring about others' opinions means being detached from their esteem and affection. This is almost impossible for people who lack self-esteem or healthy self-love because they think they are without merit or worth. The same happens with people who never received affection from family and friends and look for it from those around them.

If we receive love in childhood and adolescence, it inoculates us against emotional dependence. If we do not, like people who have experienced starvation in childhood, we are left with a permanent hunger for love that can never be satisfied no matter how much we receive, making us dependent on the good opinion of others.

Hence, we may deduce the importance of bringing up young people to develop positive self-esteem, of creating an affectionate family environment and teaching them to be good friends so as to avoid depending too much on the appreciation of others to satisfy their hunger for love.

10. Emotional independence from the outcome of our actions

The self-esteem that a person needs for his mental health is based on the esteem he perceives from others as well as his own. Both are closely connected to the outcomes of our actions. Successful people are appreciated by others and feel good about themselves; the opposite happens with losers. This makes people give a lot of importance to success and leads them to be fearful of failure. This fear can get in the way of success and produce the very failure they were dreading. People who are by nature perfectionists are prone to this and need to do everything perfectly in order to feel at ease with themselves and think they have failed if things don't turn out perfectly the first time. Such people suffer due to their intense fear of failure which paralyses unless success is guaranteed. They end up isolated and frustrated since to do things well, one has to do them badly many times first.

Not worrying too much about how our actions turn out helps us to live a peaceful life and makes it easier to aim for more worthwhile and challenging goals with a greater likelihood of attaining them since we work better when we are not afraid of doing badly. This sense of detachment comes about by not dwelling on how our action will turn out and how we will feel about the outcome. For example, when we indulge in daydreams about success, we should remember that allowing ourselves to be affected by success means we will also get more frustrated by failure. If we learn to stop dreaming about success, we will learn to stop brooding over failure, which is what brings about the fear that inhibits us from doing things well.

Emotional detachment will come more easily if we focus on doing things well, trying to overcome the obstacles that stand in the way. By so doing, it's easier to cut out memories of previous successes or failures or worrying about future outcomes, since all this distracts us and makes us commit even more mistakes.

Work and the effort to do things well, persevering with good spirits is the best way to increase our self-esteem. Much better than ideal outcomes, since these depend on external factors.

Detachment from results does not mean not bothering to aim high, since this provides the motivation that drives us to work, overcome obstacles, and forestalls discouragement with the mistakes made before achieving our target. What it means is that our desire to aim high includes love for work well done without discouragement because it guarantees that we will reach our goal.

11. We all need affection: Admit it!

From the time we are born until we die, we need to love and feel loved to be happy. We experience this when we are with people we love and whose affection we feel in return. We have already said that unconditional love for oneself is an important part of the love one needs to be happy.

The feeling of loneliness, which makes us suffer so much, has more to do with not feeling loved by others than with being physically alone.

This feeling of loneliness is even greater when someone doesn't love himself. As each one lives with himself, if he loves himself, he will be less emotionally dependent on others.

People who don't receive affection from others and don't love themselves are dissatisfied, sad, and depressed. One can understand how pets can help fill up the emptiness many people who live on their own or have few friends experience. This also explains the popularity of social networking.

The most common sources of affection are family, friends and companions, but each person has to try to deserve the love of others. This means acquiring a set of good qualities that makes one worth loving. The human being has a natural tendency to love what is beautiful, good and true. Thus, someone who wants to be loved must take care of his physical appearance (beauty) and psychological appearance (goodness and truthfulness).

In addition, to keep the love of others one must also show gratitude and know how to connect with them. Since love is shown in deeds, people who love us show it with the good things they do for us. But if we don't thank them or reciprocate, they will stop since it is hard to love an ungrateful and selfish person who takes but does not give.

From infancy we all know how to express our biological needs – hunger, thirst, sleep, rest – and to ask the help of others to satisfy them. Thanks to this we can survive physically. However, people find it difficult both to express their need for love and ask for affection.

The most plausible explanation for this reluctance is fear of:

1) admitting we need help from others and feeling inferior because we are not self-sufficient;

2) being rejected when others refuse to love us as we wish;

3) feeling indebted for the love of outsiders, whereas the love we received in the family was free;

4) feeling obliged to correspond at a high price.

Love is expressed and experienced by means of positive actions, a smile, a word of praise, a caress, being given attention, words of congratulation, a walk together, an invitation to enjoy something we like, being asked for advice, being taken into someone's confidence, being defended against wrong accusations, companionship, help in times of suffering, and so on. But it is also expressed and felt in a special way when it is said directly from the heart that one is loved a lot.

It is good to expect affection and desire expressions of love, while recognizing the reason, which is that we need love. When it is missing, we feel bad, but when we receive affection, we feel happy. Then the need and feeling of emptiness diminish, although with time they will return. This happens with all human needs and consequently we need love every day.

It is amazing to see how easily we notice our bodily, material and financial needs and how hard it is to recognize our need for love. Many people silently hope others will sense their need for affection, and then get annoyed when they don't. It seems that to admit our need for love is a shameful weakness that we need to keep hidden. To overcome this, we need to train ourselves every day to accept our need for love and ask for affection from the people who love us. In this way, we will get used to asking for affection and to giving it. Then, we must learn to correspond to the love we have been shown. In this way, love will flow more readily and everyone will be happier.

One major obstacle to the flow of love between people is the feeling of resentment for the small or big wrongs that inevitably occur when people live closely together. The antidote is a sincere and unconditional forgiveness: we have to learn to forgive and forget. This comes more easily if we start from early childhood by imitating parents and teachers who can be good models.

It is easier to learn to forgive if we have a strong desire to do so with a firm resolution to remove from our conscience any thought, memory or image related to the wrong suffered. In this way, the emotional scars fade and can be erased with an act of forgiveness. The deeper scars are usually harder to forgive, at least emotionally, even though one may very much want to.

With the present crisis in the family and the general lack of communication in the so-called communications age, the lack of affection between family and friends is leading many people to put their heart into material things, such as electronic devices, clothes, sport, cars and bikes, and animals, all of which are substitutes for human affection and cannot satisfy our need for love. Consequently, emotional dissatisfaction and feelings of loneliness are growing, and this is clearly related to the increase in both mental disorders and the consumption of stimulants and anti-depressants, as well as the increase in addictions.

12. Be critical of your feelings

Reason and Will are unique human faculties that must direct the emotions and feelings so that a person does not stray from the way of truth and goodness that leads to authentic happiness.

We have already mentioned the great influence that the feelings have. A good influence when feelings are positive and harmful when they are negative.

Some people suffer because of their intense, persistent negative feelings and emotions, which lead their mind and Will to function in a negative way. The effect of this is to produce even more negative feelings. To break this vicious circle, one has to develop the habit of being discriminating with one's feelings and avoid believing that what we feel is true, merely because we feel it.

When pessimistic people feel unhappy, they think it is because something bad is happening to them or going on in the world, but often this is not the case. By believing what they feel, they end up deceiving themselves and live a lie, which brings them into conflict with reality.

When such people feel they are failures because of their mistakes, they get really down and discouraged. Often they stop making the effort to succeed because they are convinced they cannot change the way they are. With this attitude they can never succeed and this only confirms their theory.

The same happens when they feel guilty. They feel remorse about something they have done without considering whether it was done deliberately and freely – these are the conditions for guilt. But since they feel guilty and deserving of punishment, they despise and humiliate themselves. This causes enormous suffering both to themselves and to those who love them. In extreme cases they may even believe they are responsible for everything that goes wrong and invent reasons to justify what they have done. Obviously, it's very hard for such people to be happy because they think that no-one loves them, and they reject the love shown by others since they think they don't deserve it.

Another negative feeling is inferiority. Some people believe they are inferior and therefore unlikable, and this depresses them. They spend their lives trying to do things for others so that they will appreciate them for what they do rather than what they are. These people seem unable to determine whether there are any grounds for their feeling; they assume they are inferior, but the real reason is that they were not loved when they were young.

Something similar happens with other negative feelings that make people believe things that are false: for example, feeling that others reject them makes them think the rejection is real. The fear of falling sick makes them think they are ill, like hypochondriacs; feelings of jealousy lead to the conviction that one is being betrayed; feeling unworthy of being loved makes them think that no one will love them unless they are trying to get something from them in return, etc.

These negative beliefs, derived from negative feelings, bring suffering. Since they spring from a deeply rooted character trait, they will continue in the future unless one tries very hard to root it out. Personality psychologists refer to this character trait as "neuroticism", which is at the root of mental disturbances of the "neurotic" type.

Psychologists who specialize in cognitive psychology attribute neurotic mental disturbances in patients, especially neurotic depression, now known as Dysthymia, to mistaken mental ideas about themselves or reality. They advise treating it through personal therapy.

Patients who want to change have to use their reasoning powers to analyze and criticize their negative feelings and so neutralize the power of suggestion over their Reason. For example, regarding the feeling of failure, Reason has to remember all the successes the person has achieved until then, this helps put things into perspective and stop him from feeling like a failure. With feelings of inferiority the mind must question if everyone around him is really superior. If he finds some who are obviously not, he can reject the idea of inferiority. In the face of feelings of guilt, the mind should work out whether the bad action was done voluntarily or not. In the latter case, the action is his, but he bears no guilt and should stop punishing himself.

Sometimes mental pathologies mistakes arise from positive feelings of joy, but this happens only in the most extreme cases, like euphoria or pathological elation. These occur under certain conditions, such as bipolar disorder, the influence of stimulants, such as cocaine and amphetamine, and occasionally certain medications, like corticoids, that produce ideas of grandeur or megalomania, leading to a clash with reality with the subsequent conflicts.

It is evident that feelings and emotions can influence the judgments of reason and intense emotions can distort the perception of reality. Hence the importance of developing a critical attitude towards our feelings which enables ourselves to live in the truth, be realists and adapt ourselves to changing realities.

Healthy, positive emotions help us know reality better, since they allow us to be aware of the feelings of others. Since feelings are a very important part of the person, a good understanding helps us know people better. When a normal, healthy person feels guilty, it is usually because he is guilty; when he feels inferior, it is because he is. When he feels he is a nuisance, he truly is and when he feels pity for someone, it is justified. When all is said and done, to know reality well, one needs judgment of reason regarding the truthfulness of what one feels; hence it is advisable to assess feelings critically without automatically assuming they are genuine.

13. Paradox: doing the opposite of what you intended

The paradoxical intention describes when a person obtains what he set out to achieve but at the same time he doesn't want to achieve it.

For example: things we have been frantically looking for turn up when we're not looking for them; or we recall a name or a fact we were trying to remember when we no longer need it; or someone who has been trying to get to sleep drops off when he stops trying; we perform our worst precisely when we try to do our best; or we try to make a good impression but end up looking ridiculous; or, the jealous person who doesn't want to lose the person he loves and so makes their life impossible by constantly checking up on them until they flee. The Bible also quotes paradoxes, such as "he who wants to keep his life will lose it, and he who loses his life will win it," or "the last will be first, and the first, last."

The lesson we can learn to apply in our daily lives is: to get what we want, use the strategy of not trying too hard. Don't be stubborn when something doesn't work out, leave it for later; learn how to wait for opportunities.

This will help us avoid the intense frustration that comes when things don't work out and we turn ourselves against the job in hand to the point of giving up, because it brings in its intense feelings of failure and loss of self-esteem.

Stubborn people cannot stop trying to get what they want because they are impatient and can't wait to see success. They end up blaming themselves or others for the rage caused by their frustration at their failure to get what they wanted.

In war there is what is known as strategic withdrawal or retreat, to regroup one's forces, give the troops the chance to regain their strength, and change tactics. Napoleon put it, "a timely retreat is a victory." Each person must judge if it is better to withdraw and come back later or to continue trying. If we act rationally, we can avoid pusillanimity, the opposite of obstinacy. This happens especially to weak, faint-hearted, insecure people who fear being rejected if they fail. It leads them to avoid challenges where success comes after failure.

The stubborn person is driven by his emotions and keeps up his efforts even though he knows his timing is wrong but he cannot face the frustration of failure.

It takes a lot of practice to know when to insist and when to defer until we have more idea or the circumstances are right. This kind of discernment is part of the classic virtue of prudence. As I have said before, this is easier to learn in childhood when there are good models close by, and parents and instructors who can teach it. In short, before undertaking difficult tasks, the best way to succeed is by using our Reason which has been trained to handle challenges.

14. Avoid comparisons with others

Comparing ourselves with others is a significant cause of unhappiness since we tend to make comparisons with people who are better than us. This creates the feeling of inferiority, worthlessness and failure, sadness and rejection.

This habit is often linked to two other negative traits: 1) judgment of others: making critical judgments of good people, looking for their weak points to lower their prestige in our eyes, make us feel less inferior or better than them in some way and relieve our feeling of worthlessness. 2) The tendency to compete with outstanding people so as to get the better of them and feel superior. This produces a few victories but many defeats because we cannot escape the reality of our own inferiority. The competitive attitude leads to a permanent state of tension and effort, which exhausts us physically and psychologically, causes emotional suffering, chronic stress and burn-out.

A simple way to preserve mental health is to avoid comparisons with anyone: better, worse, inferior or superior. In this way we avoid negative emotions that drive us to negative behaviors in a vicious circle.

The best is for each one to be himself and focus on what he can do best. It is a waste of precious time and energy to compare oneself with others; try to be better but avoid trying to be the best.

It is useful to remember that each one of us is unique and as persons we are far superior to any other created being: precious stones, minerals, age-old trees, and exotic animals. If we would be happy to possess such objects, it should make us much happier to know we are persons. With regard to others, we may be inferior to the best and superior to the worst, but making comparisons is futile since they don't change anything and only make us lose time that could be spent fulfilling our lives and being at peace with ourselves. This is what really matters, because we are the only ones who can live our lives and by making comparisons, we embitter ourselves. No one values a copy over an original. In other words, it is preferable to be an ordinary Tom, Dick or Harry than a superficial imitation of some important person.

Making comparisons is a difficult habit to eradicate. One way is to make use of the moments when one is under no pressure to earn appreciation, to realize one's self-worth, or when one is with family or close friends; another is to experience the enormous sensation of peace and joy when one is freed from the tension caused by comparisons. In this way one can get out of this bad habit and feel freer to be themselves, more at ease regardless of the place one occupies on the social ladder.

Parents should realize that it is harmful to compare their child with siblings or other children as a way of motivating them to perform better. This will make them develop the habit of comparing themselves with others and foster the useless desire to be better than the best. Teachers and other adults who deal with young people must avoid such comparisons so as not to foster an unhealthy competitiveness.

15. Be positive

We have already said that the characteristics of psychology depend on the characteristics of the affectivity, which in turn depend on feelings of wellbeing or discomfort, pleasure or suffering, and the attitude of the person towards them.

Learning to make progress in satisfying our physiological and psychological needs in order to achieve worthwhile objectives requires much effort and brings with it failures, conflict, and frustrations. Human beings often experience negative emotions, as we see in little children who get upset and cry for no ostensible reason. So we can safely say that one important objective of the process of psychological maturing is voluntary control of one's affectivity so that: 1) it does not react to negative stimuli with negative feelings. It is easier to begin by trying to stay calm when the stimuli are less intense because unless we can do what is easy, we won't manage to do what is difficult; 2) we can reduce the intensity and duration of the negative feelings; 3) we do not express negative feelings with behavior since this can make others suffer and make us remorseful.

Mastering this skill leads to a positive attitude in the face of suffering. The psychiatrist, Viktor Frankl, in his book "Man's Search for Meaning", expressed it in the following way: "If we are not able to change the situation, we can at least choose our own attitude towards it." The psychologist, Bernabé Tierno, repeats the same idea in the introduction to his book "Optimismo Vital" in these words: "Dear reader, you can choose to be optimistic. You can't always change events and circumstances, but you do have the power to choose how to react to them." And in his final consideration at the end of the book he says, "optimists are far less likely to fall into depression than pessimists and they tend to lead much healthier lives." Following the same idea, the psychiatrist Luis Rojas Marcos in his book The Power of Optimism, suggests two ways to foster optimism: 1) enjoy the good things of life more; and 2) adopt a positive way of thinking.

Developing a positive attitude towards suffering is a slow, costly process because it means going against the natural tendency, but it is indispensable if one has sound mental health. When someone has a strong positive attitude, he can be said to be resilient and have the strength to bear frustration.

To succeed in different areas of one's life – professional, familial, sporting, social and personal – one needs to be able to bear the sufferings these entail, because otherwise one is likely to give up the struggle and feel frustrated and defeated in life. On the other hand, unless one struggles to improve in these areas, one just gets worse since there is no stationary position: either forwards or backwards. Hence the need to struggle every day, every moment, trying not to lose one's peace and joy faced with the unpleasant facts and events of life. In this way we avoid becoming embittered and toxic.

Try to live like this: to be positive, one has to avoid being negative first. The main objective is to defend our positive feelings, our peace and joy, from negative influences. Prevention is better than cure, and this has three aspects: 1) it is easier not to get annoyed than to calm down;

2) it is easier to reject frightening thoughts from one's mind immediately than after spending time imagining possible outcomes; 3) it is easier to stop thinking straightaway about what depresses us than when we have already imagined detailed scenarios. The same applies to all negative feelings: it is easier to expel negative memories and ideas than substituting the powerful negative reactions they generate with positive feelings.

Negative people are also called toxic because they spoil the social atmosphere. They are like negativity generators. They pass on their feelings to others to find relief by talking. The human mouth is used for eating, but it can also be used for sharing bad feelings, especially anxiety, which makes people speak a lot, bite their nails, smoke, or overeat. In this way, they reduce their discomfort but without finding relief. For that you have to be a positive person.

Positive people spread good feelings to others and people like to be with them because they are good company. This makes others like them, which increases the positive and enjoyable atmosphere, whereas negative people frighten others and remain isolated, which makes things even worse, creating further unhappiness and mental illness.

16. Do not let others make you become what you don't want to be

It is good for each one to remember daily that their main objective is to be happy, and for this they must live a good life freely. But to live like this one needs a healthy, mature personality, and to achieve that, we need to avoid the negative impact of the world around us.

Humans imitate: this is a psychological phenomenon that makes it easier for us to learn from the models of behavior we see in others, models who make it easier for us to adapt to society and fit in.

Parents and educators want those entrusted to their care to behave well so they turn out to be good people who are happy. For this we need to love and be loved and since everyone loves the good, a good person is more easily loved and has more self-esteem. With this in mind, educators encourage young people to behave well and try to be role models.

In spite of the concerted efforts of parents, teachers and society to help young people turn out well, it is, unfortunately, common to come across bad people. Bad people are neither loved by others nor by themselves since they foster negative feelings: rejection, fear, hatred, and resentment. For this reason, they suffer and make others suffer.

Generally, everyone wants to be good and hopes others will be too, but many people end up being what they didn't want to be: bad people. The force driving people to be bad is negative feelings, states of mind that lead to behaviors which feel good and neutralize bad feelings, but not for long. As the bad feelings return, they are driven to worse behavior and develop bad habits and addictions, which enslave them. They then encounter unscrupulous people, who want to make quick money by distributing drugs, alcohol and pornography, deliberately corrupting others. To prevent this, educators advise young people to choose good friends, as the saying goes: "Birds of a feather, flock together."

To achieve the goal, young people must be encouraged to 1) have a clear goal of maturing into a good person 2) lay one more brick each day in the construction of this project; 3) check daily if the building is turning out according to plan so as to correct deviations in time.

Becoming the kind of person we want to be takes a daily effort so that we do not get diverted from our objective. This can happen if we get upset by others when someone treats us badly and makes us unhappy, then we respond in kind and take revenge to get our own back. The same happens when we are deceived, insulted, contradicted, humiliated, attacked, despised or rejected, our reaction is always to imitate the harm the others have done to us. In this way, bad people lead us to behave badly and gradually we become like them, when the right thing would be to ignore them.

We also allow others to corrupt us when we see that in the short run they have a good time being bad while we are having a hard time trying to be good. We feel like fools for missing out, when we see colleagues waste time at work while we are working hard, when we see others grab what they want, even things that don't belong to them while we pay for what we take; or when we see others over-eating, getting drunk, or taking drugs to escape negative emotions such as shyness, shame, fear, or sadness; or when they bully the weak to feel powerful; or when they relieve their frustration at the hardships of daily life by complaining and criticizing. Being good will make us happy in the long run. If we imitate bad role models, we end up a moaner, pessimist, hypochondriac, fearful, bitter, spoilt, vain, selfish, violent and corrupt. In this way we shall lose our freedom and independence. We become reactive, passive, not creative and consequently, no longer be able to make others happy.

The conclusion is clear, resist the negative influence of negative people very firmly if you want to reach your goal. Parents and educators have to help young people make a clear plan for being a good person who is positive and mature, and form in them a strong will to persevere in the daily challenge of progressing step by step without getting discouraged at the behavior of others.

17. Keep quiet when you are annoyed

It is quite common to see the harm which can be done with words.

With hurtful words, marriages, families, friendships and good relations between colleagues can break up. When people say hurtful things, not only does the listener suffer, but everyone around, even the speaker because sooner or later they will feel remorse and guilt.

Since prevention is better than cure, we have to think beforehand what to say to avoid hurting others, and choose words which make others feel comfortable, especially when correcting someone. Everyone knows how hard it is to speak nicely when one is annoyed. Hence the best advice is to wait before saying anything to someone who has annoyed us. As a general rule, one should always keep quiet when annoyed. If one speaks, one is sure to say something hurtful with language motivated by anger, which easily turns violent.

To manage to keep quiet when one is angry means the Will has control over the tongue. Anger is one of our basic emotions, together with fear, sadness and joy. Willpower requires constant training, which is more effective if it begins in childhood. As Aristotle said, "Man is master of his silences but the slave of his words." We have to bear the consequences of our words; if they are positive, we will feel happy with the consequences, if they are negative, we will have to endure negative consequences. "If you want to avoid saying something bad, then don't think about it." It is very advisable not to dwell on the reasons why we are annoyed because when we do, we think badly of the person, the one who annoyed us. We may not say it then, but we may at some other moment, or to someone else. In the end, our original target will get to hear of it and suffer the delayed effect.

People who struggle to be positive try to avoid speaking badly of others, they try to make positive remarks and when they cannot say something good, they keep quiet. People like this rarely hurt others but they must not forget that they easily could, so they must try to not get seriously annoyed. In the same way, it's good to keep quiet and avoid brooding when we experience intense negative emotions which make us say hurtful things. Special mention can be made of parents, who are sometimes afraid for their children and this leads them to make mistakes like using the language of threats and deception to force their children to avoid risks. Such language only makes children become insecure. When one of the parents is insecure and nervous, they should allow the other one to play a bigger role in the child's upbringing, and if both are insecure, they should ask other people who know their child well such as teachers, tutors or psychologists to help educate the child with reason and not fear.

18. *Problems are to be solved, not dramatized*

The human being is happy when he loves and possesses what is good, beautiful and true, but the way there is usually strewn with obstacles and difficulties, which require time and effort to solve.

The natural reaction when we are faced with a problem is frustration, which, for a mature person, provides the energy of Will to overcome it. When the problem seems insuperable, and one cannot get what one wants, feelings of sadness come and overwhelm and paralyze us.

This reaction is stronger in people who are results oriented because when a person's interest in the outcome is to experience peace and joy, he strives to avoid the negative influence of problems on his feelings or at least to reduce their intensity and duration.

Problems produce negative feelings. Dramatizing problems makes them more serious, more difficult, even insuperable. This produces more frustration so the person may panic each time he sees a problem, with a fear so intense that they want to run away.

To work well and acquire a positive attitude in life, it is very important to learn how to cope with problems and be optimistic when they occur. Pessimists react to problems with intensely negative emotions, particularly anger, which leads to negative behavior and suffering.

Some of the most common negative reactions when people are faced with problems are: 1) burying their head in the sand; this is no solution, unresolved problems just get bigger; 2) intense frustration and anger, physical or verbal violence towards things or people nearby, which makes others suffer and produces strong guilt feelings; 3) blaming others, usually someone good, who is ready to accept the blame and take on the problem. In this way negative people lose the chance of learning how to solve problems themselves; 4) intense sadness at not achieving their target, accompanied by discouragement, passivity, and defeatism. They give up at the first hurdle and end up with a sense of failure, leading to chronic depression.

Such negative reactions are bad example for young people. Family life, the world of work and society at large are all harmed, yet problems are a normal element in every important task and overcoming them produces satisfaction.

People who are positive and react well to problems have a high tolerance for frustrations and a good level of resilience. All personality traits are deep-rooted when practiced from childhood. Parents and educators should place tolerance of frustration and resilience among the top priorities in children's upbringing.

19. *"The best is the enemy of the good"*

Another personality trait that makes people suffer is when they want everything to be perfect: their way of being and acting; the outcome of their actions; their material and social environment and everyone else around them.

Perfectionists expect others, especially their children, to be perfect in order to love them. They try to bring up perfect children but this produces children with complexes who can never be as perfect as their parents want and instead become diffident, unsure, fearful and withdrawn.

One of the most common personality disorders in the classification of illnesses of the World Health Organization is called anankastic. In the classification of the American Psychiatric Association, it is called obsessive-compulsive. One of the key traits of this disorder is perfectionism. There are many perfectionists who don't reach this level but they still make everyone suffer.

Perfectionism is unattainable for the human being because of his natural limitations. Hence, any attempt to be completely perfect is a sure guarantee of disappointment and failure. As the saying goes, "The best is the enemy of the good." Everyday experience tells us that it is easier to love good people than "perfect" people, and as being loved makes people happy, the good find happiness more easily than the perfect.

This is the right moment to give a simple definition of a good person so as to guide the reader how to improve while avoiding perfectionism. A good person is one who feels good when he does something good. Therefore, he tries to do good whenever he can and in so doing reinforces his goodness. In the same way he feels bad when he does something bad and although he may do bad things because of his limitations, he tries to avoid them, and by struggling to avoid them he does them less. A good person feels well when he is with good people and tries to be with them as much as possible. But he feels bad when he's with bad people and tries to avoid them. He becomes good through emulating good people.

The goal of every healthy, mature person should be to try to do everything as well as possible, but knowing that first he will often do them badly, because the only way to improve is by learning from our mistakes. Doing things well, but not perfectly, has two aspects: the external, when the others see what we have done and the internal, when the person himself sees what he has done and that gives him peace of mind.

The perfectionist is usually repelled by the smallest mistake; he hates them, because for him they mean imperfection. As time goes by, he becomes incapable of starting anything unless he's absolutely sure he can do it perfectly from the start. So he lives being trapped in fixed routines where he has control over outcomes. This gives him the certainty of not making mistakes or, at least, making as few as possible. But in this way he doesn't yield the fruits which match his talents and becomes embittered.

One good piece of advice for the perfectionist is to change his objective: instead of wanting to be perfect in his actions, try to be perfect interiorly. This will help him be happy and have peace of mind, even when he is not externally "perfect". This positive feeling will affect his other mental operations, especially his Reason and his freedom, enabling him to do even external things much better.

20. Accept suffering in order to be free

Accepting means receiving and allowing something because one thinks it is good. We accept suffering without running away in order to draw benefit for ourselves and others.

Acceptance has two aspects: external and internal. Internal acceptance means avoiding reactions of rebellion. The struggle for acceptance begins with our early experience of sufferings in infancy and lasts our whole life. The moment we stop trying, our rebellion grows again. While acceptance reduces suffering and strengthens our resistance, rebellion increases suffering and can lead to phobia.

It is a question of accepting suffering, because fear makes us suffer even more than the pain we fear. If we reject suffering and run away, the fear persists and we will flee from suffering in the future so that in the end the fear becomes chronic.

Acceptance calls for persevering effort, because normally when faced with suffering we react negatively, but if we make a firm effort to accept, over time the intensity and frequency of the negative reactions will diminish.

To persevere in the struggle to accept suffering, one must start by accepting less intense sufferings early in life, because then it is easier to control negative emotions. By winning these small victories, one becomes more confident in accepting more serious suffering, although there will be occasional defeats. One should never begin with what is most difficult because then the defeats will certainly come, causing pessimism, discouragement and abandonment. Small sufferings are more common and offer more opportunities to practice, for example, delays, traffic problems, the jokes or sarcasm of others, losing objects that are not vital, misunderstandings and gaffes when dealing with others, losing sports matches, etc.

Acceptance is not the same as resignation; the first is positive and worth acquiring, the second is negative and to be avoided. Accepting suffering means to bear it with a good face: this is what has come to be known as Christian resignation, tolerance of frustration and resilience. We call this "putting on a brave face" and "not kicking against the goad." When suffering comes, non-acceptance is expressed by complaints, criticism, annoyance and sadness, which makes things even worse.

However, resignation is synonymous with passivity, of not trying to overcome the problem, obstacle or limitation that has brought the suffering.

Some people retreat from the struggle, from the effort needed and from hard work, for fear of failing since the greater the effort, the greater the disappointment. We know that with hard, constant work one is more likely to succeed. When one fails for not having tried, one suffers less since this was not real failure but a failure to engage. But this way of acting leads to laziness and passivity which prevents one from achieving worthwhile objectives. The habit of fleeing for fear of suffering defeat makes one cowardly. Fleeing from what causes fear does not remove the fear, it just accumulates. Such people go through life with a rucksack filled with fears, making it difficult for them to get ahead. It makes them chronically tired since fear generates tension, and tension produces exhaustion.

The person who habitually dominates negative reactions when facing difficulties not only feels in control of himself but also independent of his surroundings, and at ease. This self-mastery puts him in a better condition to seek higher targets, which will make him happier and improve the world around him.

21. Wasting time usefully

Success and triumph make us feel worthwhile, give us prestige, make us admired and loved. Hence the human need and drive for success.

As a result, the tendency to activism is now widespread, the "need" to do many things at the same time, multi-tasking, doing everything in a hurry, getting the maximum out of everything and competing with others.

This way of living has brought about stress, a state of psychological tension that fears failure. Stress induces wear and tear of the neurotransmitters of the brain, and can end up in depression or burn-out. It can also produce psychosomatic symptoms and illnesses owing to the physiological overload of the bodily organs.

People trapped in activism are continually thinking what they have to do next, how they have to do it and when they need to complete it to get the reward. They think less why they are doing it, if they really need to do it, or the way they are doing it and most of all, if they are happy doing it. They have neither the will nor the time to pause and reflect on these questions. For people focused on action and results, to pause and reflect is the same as doing nothing, a waste of time.

But to understand ourselves better and find happiness, a good strategy is to dedicate at least 30 minutes a day to doing nothing, in dialogue with oneself: in other words, to reflect. If we do this, we save a lot of time since mistakes can quickly be corrected. The further we travel along the wrong path, the more we move away from where we want to go and the more time we have to spend getting back to the right path.

Since the most important part of the person is the inside, we must foster a curiosity to discover our depths, encouraging reflection and interior dialogue. And so we can learn more about ourselves, and this will help us know others in depth. There are people who are amazed at how plants, animals and stars function. They marvel at the beauty of the depths of the ocean, but they have no interest in knowing how they function psychologically, and one reason is that no one has encouraged them to learn about the marvelous operations of the human mind.

Profound self-knowledge is exciting because it enables us to understand the reasons for our feelings and actions and as a result, we can live a more authentic and happier life.

To make a daily habit of reflection requires a certain degree of courage since we feel bad whenever we discover our own limitations. But we are rewarded by knowing the positive talents and qualities that make us feel worthwhile and we come to love ourselves as we are.

A simple way to begin this kind of personal examination is to ask ourselves how we feel each day and why. In this way we can get to know our emotions and feelings, which are at the core of our personality and which have enormous influence on our behavior. Knowing how these operate is essential for understanding ourselves. Initially it isn't easy to understand our feelings and so we need to ask people with more experience and knowledge, or read some books on the subject. If we find it awkward to begin with, as in any kind of training, we should still persevere because this is the key to understanding ourselves.

Since we are rational and free, in our personal dialogue we need to ask ourselves what we think about the important things of life, if we are doing things freely or are emotionally conditioned by other people. During his lifetime the human being develops mental structures which are devices to interpret reality and act within that reality. These structures are manifested in our attitude and guide our behavior.

These attitudes have three basic elements: an idea, a feeling and a way of being. Our attitudes cover every aspect of life, such as religion, work, possessions, family, sport, friendship, and so on. A positive attitude towards something brings favorable thoughts, pleasant feelings and good behavior. With a negative attitude, the opposite occurs. Knowing our attitudes and how they match reality is very important for understanding ourselves and achieving happiness by acting in the most suitable manner.

When we don't understand the reason for something that affects us, the behaviour of others or our own, we feel frustrated and upset because ignorance and doubt produce insecurity. Knowing the truth about things that affect us gives us the security that we will be able to act in the right way and avoid suffering. The strategy of reflecting every day enables us to live with more certainty, security and authenticity.

22. Learn to say "No"

Everyone knows it is not easy to say "No" to others, since this generates the fear that they will get annoyed, think we are unfeeling, and will no longer respect us, resulting in the loss of their esteem and affection.

It is very easy to say "Yes" to everything even though we may end up not doing what we promised, intentionally or otherwise. Responsible people consistently fulfil their commitments when they say "Yes". But they also need to learn to say "No", so as not to end up overwhelmed by the sheer number of promises they have made. Moreover, everyone asks them for things because they know they will do them. Unless the responsible person learns how to say "No", he usually ends up being the victim of his own success.

You learn this strategy by not replying to requests on the spot, but by waiting a few hours or even days before giving an answer. This gives one time to consider the correct reply. An answer given on the spot is usually "Yes" simply from the impulse of not wanting to feel bad.

You have to convince yourself that it is essential to be loyal to oneself, which means allowing an adequate time for reflection before answering. Since it is more difficult to say "No", the thought that this is the best for both parties can help us. One side saves himself the stress of being trapped by an unnecessary obligation that he is unable to fulfil. The other is spared the disappointment of feeling deceived after thinking the other would do the favour, or seeing that he did it reluctantly.

People who don't know how to say "No" lack the necessary emotional independence from the opinions of other people and are less able follow the dictates of their reason, something which is necessary if one is to be happy. Only by saying "No" when reason says this is the best can one recover emotional independence and freedom.

Parents can help their children in this, encouraging them to commit themselves to doing what they promise to do and to maintain their "No" when they are under pressure, or emotional blackmail from those who have asked them to do something they know they should not. Recently the expression "No means No" has become popular in the area of sexuality, but needs to be applied to all areas of daily life.

The Bible says: "Let what you say be simply 'Yes' or 'No'; anything more than this comes from evil." (Mt 5:37).

23. Practise contemplation

To contemplate is to refresh oneself, to let what one has contemplated produce a profound emotional reaction that leaves an enduring mark. One can contemplate both positive and the negative things, but to be happy and have sound mental health, it is better to focus on the positive. Everything good, beautiful, and genuine is positive.

Contemplating the positive produces lasting positive interior feelings that motivate the psychic faculties to operate positively. This leads to positive behavior that helps us and the people around us feel good. This can be seen in the eagerness of people to watch entertaining movies, read quality literature, hear good music, enjoy a tasty meal, smell fragrant aromas, see beautiful landscapes and works of art or be with people who are attractive, good and authentic.

The hardships of life generate detrimental effects which accumulate and make us act negatively. This causes worse negative feelings, creating a vicious circle which, if not reversed, ends up damaging mental health.

By producing positive effects, the daily contemplation of positive things acts like an antidote that neutralizes the impact of the inevitable hardships of ordinary life. This is a way of acquiring an interior balance and maintaining mental hygiene.

When we contemplate the good, the beautiful and the true, we acquire a taste for them and seek out people who have these qualities. Since love makes for happiness, people who have the habit of contemplation end up having a happier life. If we deal with people who are attractive, authentic and good we feel encouraged to be like them, be liked by others, and like ourselves more.

The habit of contemplation fosters sensitivity for the good and enables us to discover it in a host of little things, situations and people, neutralizing the disheartening effect of so many experiences of evil, ugliness and falsehood. Non-contemplative people are more likely to be blasé. A blasé person is one who when faced with something of wonder, doesn't even notice it and so cannot enjoy it. Such people fail to appreciate the wonder of having a spouse, of being a couple who freely decide to live together the only life they have in order to make each other happy. Or they do not marvel at the fact of having good health, of having given life to children, of having a comfortable home, a fulfilling job or friends who love them. As they don't value these wonderful realities, they don't feel the need to care for them and end up losing them and suffering when they realize they are no longer there.

The contemplative habit has another beneficial effect, it moderates activism, which can be addictive. Action has a short-term positive effect due to the increase of adrenalin in the blood. This positive effect creates a sensation of dynamism, vitality and euphoria, but it wears down the energies of the person and in the longer term, produces lethargy, lack of concentration, irritability, anxiety and sadness. As one gets older, it can end up producing burnout, which is a psychosomatic disorder.

Hence the importance of contemplation in order to have a happy life, and of teaching children to take time out for contemplation so they develop this talent. In her book Educating in Amazement, the Canadian educationalist, Catherine L'Ecuyer stresses the need to develop this capacity in children and young people to help them have a happy, positive life. What is most amazing in life is whatever beautiful, good and true, but to appreciate them, one must contemplate.

24. *Learn to laugh, especially at yourself*

In the section on not dramatizing problems, we recommended laughing at them so as to be able to resolve them better.

A sense of humor allows us to detect the amusing aspects of things around us and laugh at them. Someone with a sense of humor behaves in a carefree and entertaining way, makes others laugh and cheers them up. Moreover, he will usually have the ability to remember amusing things which he shares with others, enjoying them again in company. He prefers to look on the bright side rather than the dark and always has a funny story to tell.

Sense of humor is usually acquired in childhood and is learned by observation of an amusing relative. If not, it can be developed by watching comedies, listening to jokes and being with amusing people who see the funny side of things. Being with entertaining people gradually makes us like them.

The person with a sense of humor can convert his failures into entertaining events, which he tells other about to laugh at himself and dedramatize and neutralize any negative feelings. In this way he knows how to "look on the bright side" and lighten the load because much of our suffering comes from taking ourselves too seriously. We think: "They don't take me into account"; "they don't take notice of me", "they don't consider me", "they don't love me", "they think or speak badly of me", "they have insulted me", "they have made me wait." This egocentric attitude runs as deep as our self-love and is related to the intensity of the grudges we keep over past offenses. To keep our peace and joy we should laugh at ourselves and not listen to feelings which tell us how badly others have treated us, how unjust, how unlucky, what a bad time we have generally and how tired we are. In this way we can avoid negative feelings that rob us of our joy.

25. Don't browbeat

We sometimes come across people who feel the need to convince others that whatever they think is true, and they are always right. They do this in order to feel important. When they don't manage to convince, they interpret it to mean that the other person thinks they are wrong. Then they get annoyed and start to argue. These are people with an inferiority complex who need to reinforce their ego by feeling they are always right and showing they know everything in order to be admired and esteemed.

Everyone tends to resist having ideas forced onto them, owing to a natural love for freedom of conscience and thought. We defend this by critically analyzing the arguments of people who try to convince us. So again, we see that when one tries to convince, one brings about the exact opposite, strong resistance and heated discussion. Consequently, 'bullies' of this kind become very frustrated and annoy others by trying to coerce their freedom by arguing, in which anyone who thinks differently is abused.

To avoid this one should explain one's ideas, opinions and preferences clearly, presenting the reasons why one thinks this way but without demanding that others agree. This attitude shows respect for the freedom of conscience and ideas of others. In this way, many conflicts and misunderstandings can be avoided.

Some people are authoritative and assertive by nature and always have to compete; they have a deep-rooted habit of being controversial and argumentative and want to impose their own views. One needs to be alert to detect this quickly so as to be prepared and avoid them altogether or keep quiet and not give one's own opinions since this may only ignite a fire and start an unpleasant argument. Such people are so used to arguing that they hardly suffer at all in these situations since they are very self-centered and don't notice how uncomfortable they make others who for them, are simply verbal sparring partners. But normal people suffer a lot in such situations, so silence is the best way of avoiding arguments and showing self-control and emotional independence.

26. Sense of balance

Balance and sense of harmony denote the good. Physical imbalance can easily end in falls and broken limbs; psychical imbalance is the same as mental illness. Therefore, someone who aspires to live a good life and have sound mental health needs to struggle to acquire external and interior balance.

Perfect equilibrium is not possible and usually it is enough for it to be in due proportion. The most important thing is the balance between the negative and the positive which acts as an antidote. The negative things of ordinary life make us suffer and unless they are balanced by the positive, they can produce a permanent negative outlook, which blinds us to the positive and creates chronic suffering. It transforms someone into an embittered, frustrated, pessimistic, disappointed and depressed individual, colloquially known as a "toxic person".

It is especially advisable to acquire an adequate balance between the time one dedicates to work and rest; between the occasions when we serve others and those when we take care of ourselves; time when we are with others and time when we are alone; a time for enduring things and a time for enjoying oneself; for action and contemplation, for speaking and for listening, for sleeping and being awake, for rest and physical exercise, for obligations and for devotions, for duty and leisure. As in other aspects of human life, we must use our Reason to decide what is to be done to achieve this vital balance, and reason needs time to reflect on the way we live and the way we ought to live. Lastly, we rely on a strong will to put our reasoned conclusions into practice.

The person who is well-balanced feels in control of his own life and experiences freedom; this will never be complete, but it will be enough for him to feel happy with himself.

27. A flexible mind

The world around us is changing all the time. To be happy, a person needs to be able to assimilate these changes. When someone doesn't or can't adapt, he will be maladjusted. When someone manages to adapt quickly, he is said to be psychologically flexible.

Mental flexibility is closely related to intelligence, which perceives changes, grasps the reasons and then quickly adopts a positive attitude that enables him to attain his objectives. Intelligent people are usually more flexible, but to adapt well, one also needs the intellectual habit called creativity, which enables one to appreciate different perspectives and find new ways to function.

Mental flexibility also depends on how well the will controls the feelings. Some people are very sensitive and have intense, long-lasting emotions which exercise a powerful influence over their minds. They are trapped in a positive or negative mindset according to the emotion they feel. This tends to reduce their mental flexibility and capacity to adapt. For example, there are many people who feel good relaxing, e.g., listening to music, watching a TV series, playing video games or cards and are then incapable of stopping, even though they know they have other duties to fulfil. Their feelings do not allow them to feel comfortable doing something which takes more effort and which they do not like so much. There are others who, when they are annoyed, behave violently and are unable to recover their equanimity, even though they know they are making their loved ones suffer. These are people who, when they are afraid, they are unable to confront what is making them afraid, or when they feel shame, they cannot avoid hiding or running away from social situations. They persist in trying to solve a problem that has no solution or carrying on an endless discussion because they do not want to feel bad by not getting their point across. Such people cannot tolerate having to wait, or tolerate doubt, uncertainty or fear. They keep pestering others to rescue from such situations, although they realize they are only making a nuisance of themselves, or what they are asking for is impossible.

Flexibility is a personality trait that facilitates adaptation to changing circumstances and other people's different ways of being. It minimizes conflicts and the suffering that every lack of adaptation brings about. This trait combines flexibility of reason and emotions and when the two come together, they contribute to the quality that has come to be known as "emotional intelligence", which involves a coordination of the intelligence and the feelings, leading to a more positive and creative way of living.

Like every personality trait, flexibility is acquired early in life through repeated practice. This training comes from parents who are good models and who know how to give in to the demands of their children when these are reasonable. They are willing to recognize their own mistakes and shortcomings; they change their way of acting when this is good for the children; they give up family routines when the family needs this; they stop doing what they are doing when there is an important need or those in their care need the change; they modify their timetable if others ask and their request is fair.

Being mentally flexibility is not to be confused with being unreliable, changeable or easily discouraged. These indicate emotional dependence on favourable circumstances and lack of fortitude to persevere in one's personal objectives and convictions.

28. Self-reference

Self-reference means talking to excess about yourself and your doings. So, we define it as a psychological phenomenon whereby a person interprets everything around him in reference to himself as if the world revolved around him.

Self-reference is the consequence of inflation of the Ego and people like this are called egocentric. Technically this is called positive self-reference where the subject thinks that the world functions thanks to him; that they are somehow involved in everything good that happens around them: tasks turn out well thanks to them; matches are won through them, the family remains united or is financially prosperous through his efforts, relationships are successful because of his sacrifices, etc. Such people are unable to see the positive things of other people, whom they despise in order to feel superior. Over time they also lose out when others pay them back with the same coin: contempt and rejection. In more serious cases they manifest delusions of grandeur, as in bipolar disorder.

Negative self-reference affects both those who suffer it and their loved ones who feel helpless to alleviate their pain. The people close to them see them suffer continually without being able to assist them. This kind of self-reference makes the person interpret everything around him as negative and harmful. They think that if something goes badly, it is their fault, that others think badly of them, that nobody loves them, that they are a nuisance, that they are in the way, that they cause others to suffer and that they are making others waste time with their needs and requests. This kind of self-reference is a characteristic of personality disorders and also a symptom of psychosis. In more serious cases, negative self-reference psychosis becomes paranoid delusions, which are firm convictions of false realities, often associated with "paranoid delirium" in paranoid psychotics. Less serious forms are inferiority complex and predisposition to neuroses of anxiety and depression.

People with negative self-reference are like "a black hole" that attracts everything around it, like the color black that absorbs all light and heat waves. They have a negative personality core owing to their low self-esteem and intense inferiority complex which makes them see themselves as black sheep or ugly ducklings with neither dignity nor rights, deserving of harsh treatment and contempt. The negative vision they have of themselves makes them project onto the world their own negative ideas and to expect the worst of their fears to come true. Their negative feelings (inferiority, insecurity and fear) distort their perception of themselves, of reality around them and makes them act in a destructive way, which in turn only brings about what they fear: rejection, guilt, humiliation, abandonment, and criticism, thus confirming their negative convictions.

People who are conditioned by negative self-referencing don't feel free to act. They may try to behave in a way that has a positive influence on their immediate environment so as to compensate for their negative input and end their isolation.

It is very difficult for such people to change; helping them is a never-ending task because to change radically, they would have to be born afresh. The only way to change is to help them discover their good qualities, increase their self-esteem and reduce or eradicate their feelings of inferiority which generate their negative self-image and which they try to have confirmed by others. It is best to begin by encouraging them to cast out negative self-referential thoughts from their conscience or at least try to do so. If they do, they will develop the willpower to control their thoughts about themselves and avoid the negative emotions that induce negative self-reference in the first place.

Given the difficulty of curing negative self-reference, one sees how necessary it is to insist on the importance of giving children a positive upbringing, discovering their good qualities and rewarding positive behavior rather than punishing the negative ones. A positive upbringing fosters self-esteem, which is the foundation of a mature and healthy personality.

29. True freedom: needs, duties and desires

Freedom, doing things "because one feels like it", is a necessary condition for happiness. People who are conditioned to live in a certain way are not happy. Similarly, people with addictions see their freedom reduced and are unhappy.

Because of their personality, some people create permanent needs and duties for themselves. Consequently, they feel trapped and their freedom restricted, which prevents them from finding happiness.

Needs are natural or acquired, biological or psychological insufficiencies. They come with a feeling of discomfort proportional to the intensity of the need, which drives the person to satisfy the need. This brings pleasure and a feeling of well-being.

Natural needs are common to every person, though with differences of intensity, tolerance and degree of incitement to their satisfaction. Some examples of biological needs are: hunger, thirst, sleep, the sexual appetite, relaxation and rest. Some natural psychological needs are: security, self-esteem, competence, love, curiosity, company, intimacy, enjoyment and inclusion in a social group.

Among the acquired needs, the difference between people is greater since they depend on the habits and unique experiences of each individual. From the examples listed above and below, it is clear that individual needs vary; also, there are different levels of intensity. There is the need to smoke, to drink alcohol, coffee or stimulating drinks, medicines or drugs; to eat at certain hours or certain types of food; to listen to certain kinds of music, read certain books, check out new technologies, watch certain programs or shows; the need to speak, act, do exercise, be with certain people, be the center of attention and to be in the right; the need for order, punctuality, the need to let off steam by complaining.

To defend one's freedom, one needs to reflect from time to time on one's needs and their intensity so as to reduce our dependency on them when our reason tells us to. Likewise, it is better to avoid creating new needs; some people transform their dreams, whims and tastes into needs: I must have a new car, a more comfortable bed, more fashionable glasses, a more powerful computer, a better chair for my back. Then, they do nothing but think how they are going to satisfy these needs so as to feel good. As they satisfy them, they create new ones and so they never get out of the vicious circle of need –

satisfaction – need – satisfaction… which takes away their freedom and leaves them perpetually dissatisfied.

Hyper-responsible people consider all the tasks they do in their family, social and work environments as duties even though they may have no obligation to do them. They feel compelled to help others fulfil their obligations. Any tasks left undone make them feel bad, and once they are completed, they feel relieved, a feeling which doesn't last long because it is quickly replaced by a feeling of discomfort as new duties seem to crop up. People like this become trapped in the vicious circle of duty, discomfort, fulfilment of duty, well-being, new duty. This limits their freedom and happiness. To avoid it, they have to foster the habit of self-examination and put a brake on their tendency to create duties for themselves.

The term "want" means a free decision of the will. When someone does things because he wants to, he develops his freedom and personal autonomy and is therefore happier. If the things he wants are good, his decisions contribute to his personal growth. Because he is free, it is easier to rectify when he realizes he has gone wrong, or he lacks the ability to do something. On the other hand, it is not easy for the person driven by need and duty to rectify because he will feel bad at leaving something undone and feel he has failed to fulfill his duty.

As we have seen, sound mental health means controlling one's thoughts and language to change the concepts of need or duty to free desires, which are acts of the will, trying to do what is needed or what has to be done because one wishes to do it; that is, even when you have no choice because it has to be done, you try to make it a voluntary choice, freely taken on.

30. A healthy mind in a healthy body

In all ages of Man and especially in present-day Western society, the human being has counted on bodily sensations to feel well good since there is a close relationship between the psyche and the soma, which the Roman poet, Juvenal, immortalized in one of his Satires: mens sana in corpore sano (a healthy mind in a healthy body).

People look for the pleasant and pleasurable sensations that accompany eating, drinking and sleeping; sexuality, relaxation, sports, swimming and massage; seeing, hearing, smelling and touching; smoking or taking drugs, nice clothes, decorating the body: tattoos, piercing, suntans, make-up, slimming and surgical modifications. We can also include taking medication to relieve symptoms of physical illnesses such as pain, anxiety, and insomnia, in order to feel well again.

To maintain the balance proper to mental health, the mind and will must regulate the use of the body to feel well; in this way one prevents the trauma caused by addictions or obsessions. These are produced when the feelings control the mind-body relationship since their objective is to feel good or less bad in the present moment, without taking into account the longer-term consequences.

The body is necessary for life, but the main purpose of life is happiness, one's own and that of those we love. This is only attained when one loves and is loved in return. To be loved, one needs to be good, since we desire what is good and reject what is bad; and to be good we have to behave well. Behaving well takes effort and requires a strong will to restrain our impulse to misbehave to achieve a fleeting satisfaction. A strong will drives us to do good, which makes us happy in the longer term: strong willpower helps free us.

So, love, goodness, freedom and happiness are all closely related. But pleasure, pleasurable sensations, addictions and unhappiness are also closely related. To be happy and enjoy mental and physical health, one must empower the first group and reduce the second.

When people value someone, they respect him and treat him according to the laws of his nature. To avoid physical and mental ills, one must emphasize the great dignity of the human body, since this has to do with human life and is something sacred. Things are sacred when related to God, and life has been considered a gift of God throughout history. Thus, the body, as the basis of life, is also sacred and must be treated with great respect. The human right to life derives from the sacredness of the body as does the corresponding duty to not abuse it.

Epilogue

The human being is happy when he does what he has to and does it freely because he feels like doing it.

To do things well, first we have to do them badly many times, and since failures cause disappointment, there are people who avoid taking action and prefer to be passive. They do not reach the perfection which they are destined to by their natural talents and they live an unfulfilled life.

To be able to do things freely it is necessary to develop one's will, which means to have a willpower, which is directly proportional to one's freedom. Our strength increases when we do things that are hard or even unpleasant, but we do them because they are good and worthwhile. Since everything unpleasant involves some suffering, many people try to avoid them but they fail to develop their willpower and so lack the freedom they need. They look to other people to make decisions for them and become dependent and unhappy.

Consequently, people who always choose what is pleasant and reject the unpleasant develop a passive-dependent personality, which makes everyone suffer. When others don't live up to their expectations, they feel intense frustration, and they castigate them. Such people manipulate others and develop a passive-aggressive personality.

So, there is a close relationship between passive-dependent and passive-aggressive, both are pathological and bring suffering.

One must learn from childhood how to live in a way that makes one ever better and freer so as to live a happy life because there are no second chances. Although one can always rectify, because the human being always retains a spark of freedom, it takes much more effort to rectify than to learn to do things well from the beginning.

Apart from discussing the importance of making a daily effort to cultivate the mind and have harmony between reason and the emotions, this book also provides some psychological and practical strategies and tips for achieving this.

These are the fruits of many years spent trying to help people undergoing the psychological suffering caused by mental illness.

Bibliography

BINSWANGER, L., *Being-in-the-world*, Basic Books, New York, 1963.

FRANKL, V., *Man's search for meaning*, 3rd edition, Ed. Herder, Barcelona 2015.

GÓNGORA, L., *Tesoro de los romanceros y cancioneros españoles, históricos, caballeres- cos, moriscos y otros, recogidos y ordenados por Don Eugenio de Ochoa*, Libería de Pons y Compañía, Barcelona 1840.

ROJAS, E., *¿Quién eres?: De la personalidad a la autoestima*. Ed. Temas de Hoy, S.A., Madrid 2001.

ROJAS, L., *The power of optimism*, Ed. Santillana, Madrid 2005.

SARRAIS, F., *Personalidad*, Ed. Eunsa, Pamplona 2012.

TIERNO, B., *Optimismo vital*, Ed. Temas de hoy, Madrid 2007.

<table>
<tr><td>Title:</td><td>30 Tips for a Happy Life</td></tr>
<tr><td>Author:</td><td>Fernando Sarráis</td></tr>
<tr><td>Translated from:</td><td>30 Consejos para una vida feliz (Spanish)</td></tr>
<tr><td>Translator:</td><td>Martyn Drakard</td></tr>
<tr><td>Authorization:</td><td>Ediciones Palabra, S.A., 2021</td></tr>
<tr><td>Published by:</td><td>Spring Publications Limited
103 Austin Road, Tsimshatsui
Kowloon, Hong Kong
Website: http://www.spring-books.com
Email: info@spring-books.com</td></tr>
</table>

ISBN: 978-988-79408-6-9

www.ingramcontent.com/pod-product-compliance
Lightning Source LLC
Chambersburg PA
CBHW050534160726
48003CB00002B/588